RESPECT THE S.W.A.G.

The Official Guide To the only S.W.A.G. that Matters

I'm So Educated™ Founder Michael Mallery Jr.

Contents:

Contents:

About the Author:

Entrepreneur, Motivational Speaker, Mentor, Visionary, and Humanitarian, are just a few titles of distinction used to describe Michael Mallery Jr., who is known today as one of the freshest and most respected young-leaders around. While being the CEO of his own company, his collective work and influence in the world clearly exhibits his passion and purpose for inspiring the next wave of young students to greatness. Michael has helped and motivated thousands of students to attend colleges and universities around the country.

Born and raised in Louisiana, Michael has been able to work with two of the world's leading companies: 3M Company and Wal-Mart Stores Inc., in addition to marketing products for the internationally known Mcilhenny Company's (Tabasco®). Throughout the past 5 years, Michael's scholastic achievements and electrifying presentations has allowed him to inspire and educate young professionals all throughout the country. Michael has captivated audiences ranging from Fortune 500 Companies and CEO's, down to higher and lower educational institutions.

Acknowledgments:

This book, like everything else I have created in my life, is the result of the love and support of my family and mentors. I want to thank my siblings Michaela, John, and Jayna for always lending an ear and for all of their support throughout the years. I love you all.

Now, I would like to extend my deepest gratitude and thanks to my parents:

Helen Mallery, my loving mother who has always believed in me. I'm honored to have such an incredible woman in my life that cares for me and will always be there for me no matter what. Mom, thank you for all of your support. I love you very much.

Michael Mallery Sr., my incredible father who has believed and invested in my dreams from day one. In a world where so many young men are growing up without their fathers, I am honored that my father has been there for me and continues to believe in my dreams. Pops, I want to thank you for all of your advice and all of your love. You were right my day in the sun is finally here, so I'm going to make the most out of it.

Also, final thanks to all of my business partners and mentors who have challenged me and have made this life of mine worth living, Ms. Lauri Patterson, Mr. Greg Davis, Mr. Joe Cotton, Mr. Phillip James, Mr. Ronald Alexander. Mr. Armando Jimenez, Mr. Aaron Miller, Ms. Shantel Honeyghan, Mr. Joshua DuBois, Mr. Brandon Frame, Ms. Seanice DeShields, Mr. Damarcus Alexander, Mr. Devin Addison, Mr. Edwardo Rangel. If I missed anyone, I do apologize. I am very grateful for you all and my prayer is that GOD continues to bless you all.

This book is dedicated to all of the Students throughout the world who have ever dared to meet their hearts desires. I believe in you and I want to thank you for believing in yourself. I salute each of you who RESPECT the S.W.A.G., who LOVE the S.W.A.G., and those who aim to BECOME the S.W.A.G.

Foreword:

There are countless stories of the powerful role that education has played in opening new, exciting pathways to life. Millions of people from South Carolina to the South Bronx have testimonials to this fact. One of my favorite stories comes from the Atlanta, where there was a young man with little resources, a single parent home and tendencies to run the streets in a hopeless, nihilistic and painfully troubled way. Let's call him Joe.

Joe and his friends robbed and assaulted people, sold drugs, and proved little more than a menace to themselves and others. If someone had made a prediction, the odds were that, their near futures would be painfully bleak. In fact, drug dealers exponentially increase their odds of being shot, stabbed, beaten, arrested, raped (yes raped), murdered, stripped of the right to vote, and living in poverty. (These rates are also higher for high school drop outs, although not as dramatically so.) Joe, however, changed his odds by joining the military, but at the risk of being discharged dishonorably, decided to attend college on the G.I. Bill. Unable to leave the street life alone, Joe robbed and assaulted people the summer before he started college. Once on campus, he continued to sell drugs. But…the exposure to a new world of ideas forged a new identity in the young man.

His exposure to new ideas and perspectives on the world caused an indelible imprint on his worldviews. From professors, to fellow students, to guest lecturers at the College, Joe was inspired to view his own life as bound into a broader fabric of humanity. The chant "Free Nelson Mandela" struck a chord. Who was this black militant locked away for over a quarter of a century in South Africa?

He was viscerally affected by the massive resistance against Apartheid in South Africa. He was inspired by the images of young people—his age—who risked their lives in the shantytowns of Soweto. From this he grew fascinated by history. It informed him of the world in which he lived. It provided context for not only South Africa, but Southwest Atlanta, South Central Los Angeles, and the Southside of Chicago and the Global South. He became a history major, an activist, a student leader, and graduated with Latin Honors. Today, he is an alumnus of a top law school, and the married father of five children. He founded a law firm in the D.C. area and was awarded work for his pro bono efforts. He has travelled to multiple continents, mentors and volunteers in the community.

The opportunities and life experiences have been a direct consequence of the transformation afforded him when he walked onto campus as a freshman. To paraphrase George Washington Carver, education was the key that unlocked Joe's golden door of freedom.

The value of education can be quantified in a myriad of ways. Typically, income is the measurement of choice. Over the course of one's life, a college graduate earns over $1.5 million over one with only a high school diploma, and more than $2.2 million more than a high school dropout. The numbers only improve from there. Using a high school diploma as a benchmark, on average, one earns an extra $2 million with a master's, and almost $3 million with a professional degree (R.N., J.D., or M.D.). The benefits are not limited to increases in lifetime earnings. One is much less likely to be unemployed, as expected. During the recession of 2010, the national unemployment rate reached

8.2 percent, but those without a high school diploma and high school grads have the highest unemployment rates—a staggering 15 percent. But those with a college degree had a rate of 5.4 percent. Those with a professional degree had an even lower rate—2.4 percent. Doctorate degree holders were what economists call "full employment" at only 1.9 percent unemployment. While a Ph.D. may or may not be in your future, education unquestionably provides greater opportunities for financial rewards the more you have.

But beyond the financial rewards—millions of dollars over a lifetime—that one can get from a college degree and advanced degree, the quality of one's life is enhanced in innumerable ways. Studies confirm that people who have a college degree live longer than those without. They are more physically active; they are actually happier. And, finally, education can help you change the world.

Malcolm X never finished high school before he went to prison. It was there, however, where he converted to Islam, and read voraciously. He attended classes in prison, honed his skills as an orator and debater. He would famously say that, "education is our passport to the future, for tomorrow belongs to those who prepare for it today." But, while education can open doors, the call to leave the world better than you find it is also a powerful one. And education becomes an indispensable tool. Human rights leader and iconic soldier for freedom and justice Nelson Mandela insisted that education alone would was no guarantee for moral or ethical leadership. He states, "[a] good head and good heart are always a formidable combination. But when you add to that a literate tongue or pen, then you have something very special."

Within the pages of the book you are holding, Michael Mallery provides an easy, accessible guide to students who want to achieve, maximize, push themselves, excel and grind. This is easy in many respects, but like anything, it takes effort, attention and drive. Thousands of young people make decisions to commit to a range of things. Expertise in most of things does not come without some effort. One is not instantly great at baseball, ballet, engineering, writing, hockey, physics, or football. The best physicists may have been mediocre students in history. Perhaps Wayne Gretsky, the best hockey player of all time, was poor in football. Still, his effort in hockey is what made him great.

It is always about focus, hard work and, importantly, establishing goals. Discover your passion. The greats did not give up when they found themselves mediocre in one field. Nor did they stop when they were not deemed the greatest in their chosen one. Find your strength. Find your art, subject, skill, and cultivate it. Nourish it and watch it grow. Establish your goals and dare to be amazing. Dare to be bold. Unlock your own golden door.

Dr. Jeffrey O. G. Ogbar
Vice Provost for Diversity
Professor of History
University of Connecticut

Congratulations. If you are reading this book, you have looked inside of your heart and you believe that becoming the **S**tudent **W**ith **A**cademic **G**oals is extremely important on your journey to success.

For starters, I believe in YOU. If no one in your life has ever spoke those words into your life, let me do so again.

I BELIEVE IN YOU! I BELIEVE IN YOU! I BELIEVE IN YOU!

My fellow student, I believe in you, I believe in your future, and I definitely believe in all of those amazing dreams you have. I don't have to know you personally to recognize that you are filled with so much potential.

Let me ask you a question, **what do you want to be in your life?** Take a second and think about that. **Ask yourself,** what do I want to be in life? Maybe you want to be a Doctor, a lawyer, a pediatrician, an engineer, a writer, a painter, an entrepreneur, a banker, or even the President of the United States. Hey, if you don't know right now, that's perfectly fine, however, do you believe in SWAG?

You may not be the **S.W.A.G.**, but if you believe in the **S.W.A.G.**, you can certainly become the **S.W.A.G**. So ask yourself, can I become the SWAG? If yes, then I believe you are in for one incredible read that will help you understand why becoming the SWAG is so crucial in your life.

My friends and fellow students sit back and enjoy, as it is my high honor and privilege to give you the only **S.W.A.G.** that matters.

-Michael Mallery Jr.
Founder and CEO of I'm So Educated™
www.imsoeducated.com

Introduction:

This is not a book of good concepts. This is a book of endless philosophies used by successful men and women throughout history. I have studied these success principles for over 15 years and have applied them to my own life. The incredible level of achievement that I now enjoy is the result of applying these principles day in and day out for the past 15 years of my life.

Now I would love to take credit for the SWAG that I do have. But the truth is, the SWAG was given to me, by my grandmothers, may they continue to rest in peace.

You see my grandmothers, both born in Louisiana, were literally the smartest people I ever knew, one born in 1926 and the other born in 1933. During that time, my grandmothers and minority women were considered second class citizens, many did not have the economic means to learn pass the six grade. So in other words, after six grade they had to get a job. Now you may be wondering, how could they have been the smartest people you knew if they did not get pass the sixth grade. My answer to you is simple, they never stopped educating themselves. They told me, the only way you're going to make it in this world, is by becoming a **S**tudent **W**ith **A**cademic **G**oals.

My grandmothers gave me at the very young age of 9, many SWAG tips that I will be sharing with you throughout this book.

Applying these S.W.A.G. tips and principles has allowed me to experience so much success in and out of the classroom. I have inspired and motivated thousands of students across the country to attend colleges and universities, I am the Founder and CEO of I'm So Educated™ Student Enrichment Seminars, a Boy Scout of America Eagle Scout, 2011 National Public Speaker Winner sponsored by Enterprise Rent-A-Car and Pi Sigma Epsilon Business Fraternity, inducted in to Beta Gamma Sigma Business Honor Society, 2011 National B.E.E.P (Black Executive Exchange Program 1st Place Marketing Case Competition Winner, 2011 Pi Sigma Epsilon Southwest Regional ADP Company Case Competition Winner, 2011 Gala on the Bluff Scholarship Recipient 2010 Mcilhenny Co. Tabasco® Social Media Challenge Winner, 3M Company Team Leader on Corporate Brand Personality Research Project, Collegiate Academic Dean's List, 3M Company Sales Scholarship Recipent,

WHAT IS SWAG?

Before you can respect the S.W.A.G. and become the S.W.A.G., you first have to ask yourself what is SWAG?

How do you define SWAG? (Fill in your definition of SWAG)

_____

_____

_____

_____

_____

_____

Now that you have your definition of what SWAG is, let me give you a smoother definition that summarizes it.

SWAG **-One that possesses style, personality, and an abundance of confidence.**

The goal of this book is to redefine the SWAG that you have or that you think you have, and educate you on the only S.W.A.G. that matters. Which you should be processing into your mind, body, and soul by now, which is....

Students With Academic Goals.

Now let's break the word **SWAG** down for further clarification.

What is a student?

Well according to dictionary.com a **student** is
"a person formally engaged in learning, or any person who
studies, investigates, or examines thoughtfully"

Key Take Away: **Someone who learns!!!**

With
  "characterized by or having"

Key Take Away: **Having**

Academic
  "pertaining to areas of study, learned or scholarly"

Key Take Away: **Learned and study**

Goals:
"the result or achievement toward which effort is directed"

Key Take Away: **Achievement and effort**

Always remember this, Societies SWAG helps you get into the game, my S.W.A.G. is designed for you to understand the Game.

Before we get started, I think we should separate the pretenders from the contenders.

Before you proceed through this book I need those serious about Becoming the S.W.A.G. to recite this affirmation and sign your signature at the bottom of it.

Today is my moment and now is my time

To believe in my dreams and go after what's mine

I pledge to myself I will ignore the haters

To rise above and achieve what's greater

No One, I repeat, No one, will ever stop me from reaching my dreams

Because *I'm So Educated™, I'm So Educated™, I'm So Educated™*

*Name:*_____

If you recited that affirmation and signed your signature, then my friends and fellow students, you are ready to learn what becoming the S.W.A.G. can do for you.

S.W.A.G.

Starting Point

Alright let's get started.

Ask yourself these questions so you can begin your journey of first Respecting the S.W.A.G.

Answer the following Questions

What do I want to be?_____

_____

_____

Am I satisfied with the student I am?_____

_____

What motivates me?_____

_____

Who believes in me?_____

_____

_____

How much money do I want to make?_____

_____

What parts of learning do I enjoy the most?_____

_____

_____

What are the most important things to me in life?_____

_____

_____

How do I describe myself?_____

_____

_____

Do I need an education for what I want to do in my life?__

_____

_____

Why is it that some students care about their education while others do not?

_____

_____

_____

What are your biggest goals and dreams?_____

_____

_____

_____

Answering those questions was the next step in becoming the S.W.A.G. because it allowed you to look inside of yourself and reflect on what it is that you want. That's a very **POWERFUL** next step. My hope for you is that after you answered the questions, you realized that you deserve more and that it is time to put in work.

Dream Building

{See YOUR Future, Build YOUR Future}

One of the most important things you can do for yourself right now as a student, is begin to dream build. **Dream Building** is having pictures of things you want to eventually have, achieve, people whose lives you want to touch, and places you want to go.

Dream building keeps you focused on your future and constantly reminds you that **only you** control the future. Dream building inspires you to work hard and to **LEARN** how to acquire those things the right way.

In order to have a nice car or house or inspire the world, you do not have to have it right now, you just have to see it.

Dream building reminds you that you are capable of getting whatever you want out of life.

Financial Goals:
Look at this EVERY single day

What are my financial goals?_____

_____

How much do I want to save?

1 Year _____

5 Years _____

10 Years _____

Cut out a picture of it and place it below.

Financial Goals

Place Photo in between lines.

_____

_____

Dream place to Live:
Look at this EVERY single day

Where is my dream place to live in?_____

Cut out a picture of it and place it below.

Dream Location

Place Photo in between lines.

_____

_____

<u>Dream Car:</u>
Look at this EVERY single day

What is my dream car?_____

How much does it cost?_____

Cut out a picture of it and place it below.

Place Photo in between lines.

_____

_____

Dream House:
Look at this EVERY single day

What does my dream house look like?_____

How much does it cost?_____

Cut out a picture of it and place it below.

Place Photo in between lines.

_____

_____

<u>Dream Job:</u>
Look at this EVERY single day***

What is my dream job?_____

Cut out a picture of it and place it below.

Place Photo in between lines.

_____

_____

Dream organization to volunteer for:
Look at this EVERY single day

Where do I want to volunteer?_____

Cut out a picture of it and place it below.

Place Photo in between lines.

_____

_____

__Dream place to visit:__
Look at this EVERY single day

Where do I want to visit?_____

How much does it cost?_____

Cut out a picture of it and place it below.

Place Photo in between lines.

_____

_____

S.W.A.G.

IS

IN

SESSION!!!

50 TIPS TO BECOMING THE S.W.A.G.

S.W.A.G. REALITY

Here is the reality:
You have the potential to become as successful as you want to be. It is very important to ask yourself questions that will allow you to stay focused on your goals in life. I know it is hard, but please do not buy into the **MYTH** that success comes easy. Do not believe everything you see from celebrities, television, or social media sites because the real truth is that there are no LIGHTS or CAMERA without ACTION!!!! Trust me, you need to have an education in order to become successful in this world.

**If you do not remember anything else from this book,
It is important that you
NEVER FORGET
This one line!!!**

<u>YOU NEED TO HAVE AN EDUCATION IN ORDER TO BE SUCCESSFUL IN THIS WORLD.</u>

These 50 tips are designed to build practice on the skills you want to create and give you insight on how to improve your education by using effective skills that many other successful students have implemented in their lives. The fact remains that in order to become the SWAG you have to respect the SWAG.

S.W.A.G. TIP #1
Start where you are

It does not matter where you are, what your grades may be, or if people have counted you out, as long as you believe that when your dream is big enough your odds don't matter, you can become successful.

S.W.A.G. TIP #2
Circle of TRUTH

Whoever you surround yourself with is who you will become. Ask yourself one question, "Is the circle of people I surround myself with enhancing my life?" Or wasting my time?

If the answer is that they are wasting your time, then you have to love them from a distance. The truth is you will lose friends and people will talk about you, however if you really believe that you can become the successful person you are, then you have to make changes to your circle.

S.W.A.G. REFLECTION:

What did I learn?

_____

_____

_____

_____

_____

Will I use these tips? (Circle One)   Yes   Maybe   No

Notes:_____

_____

_____

_____

_____

_____

_____

_____

_____

S.W.A.G. TIP #3
Get a notebook

To become the S.W.A.G. you have to track your daily performance. Most successful students have a notebook to track their performance. From taking notes, jottings down ideas, and writing out a plan to do better, the S.W.A.G. who has a notebook, boost their productivity significantly because they are consistently looking at ways to improve themselves. What matters the most is that you write important things down and visually reflect on it. That will help you see your results from today, ponder ideas for tomorrow, and map out goals for the week.

S.W.A.G. TIP #4
Get Organized

A key characteristic in most successful students is that they are all organized.
Get organized by creating assignment folders, writing in a calendar, and having different notebooks for each class. When you're organized, you are able to accomplish more work.

S.W.A.G. REFLECTION:

What did I learn?

_____

_____

_____

_____

_____

Will I use these tips? (Circle One)   Yes   Maybe   No

Notes:_____

_____

_____

_____

_____

_____

_____

_____

_____

S.W.A.G. TIP #5
Goals

What are your goals? To become a better student you have to know what you're striving for. It is critical that you write out what it is that you want to achieve.

Create a goals book. (see page 113) 30 day goal jump start

S.W.A.G. TIP #6
Visualize Success Daily

One of the most useful techniques for becoming successful is to simply close your eyes and visualize what you want to accomplish. Visualize your success and then get out there and make it happen.

S.W.A.G. REFLECTION:

What did I learn?

_____

_____

_____

_____

_____

Will I use these tips? (Circle One)   Yes   Maybe   No

Notes:_____

_____

_____

_____

_____

_____

_____

_____

S.W.A.G. TIP #7
Finish with a Positive

At the end of every class period, study session and practice, end on a good note. You can do this by reworking a problem you know the answer to or reciting a definition you have memorized. This is important because it allows you to end on a positive note of success.

S.W.A.G. TIP #8
We are what we repeatedly do

Embrace repetition. Students with academic goals understand that success comes from constantly working and reworking problems. Repetition is the single most influential thing we can do to improve our skills. It helps sharpen our skills and retain more information. For example, two of the world's biggest stars Michael Jordan and Michael Jackson could not have become great stars without repetition. Had they not have worked for hours and hours on their craft, they would not have become legendary.

S.W.A.G. REFLECTION:

What did I learn?

_____

_____

_____

_____

_____

Will I use these tips? (Circle One)   Yes   Maybe   No

Notes:_____

_____

_____

_____

_____

_____

_____

_____

S.W.A.G. TIP #9
15 Minutes A day

What is the best way to expand your mind? Is it by listening solely to a teacher's lesson? Reading an instructional book? Absolutely not!!! It is about getting out there and trying out something new. Do not be afraid to try something new, even if it is intimidating. That is how you begin to build new skills and broaden your horizon. Block off 15 minutes every day and try something new or visit a new idea.

S.W.A.G. TIP #10
Don't be afraid to fail

How many perfect people do you know? If the answer is NONE, than now is the time to give up your fear of failing. Listen to me; you have to be prepared to push yourself to the boundaries of what others deem as impossible. To become the S.W.A.G. you have to be willing to apply yourself and work as hard as you can to make that happen. Now yes, it is true that even when you work as hard as you can, you may fail or sometimes look silly to others, however, even in your failures you still cannot escape learning.

Remember, all of the brilliant minds, greatest athletes, and celebrities have failed at something before, but they persevered and became legendary.

Repeat this... "Even if I fail, I'm So Educated™"

S.W.A.G. REFLECTION:

What did I learn?

_____

_____

_____

_____

_____

Will I use these tips? (Circle One)   Yes   Maybe   No

Notes:_____

_____

_____

_____

_____

_____

_____

_____

S.W.A.G. TIP #11
Build RELIABLE Skills

To develop reliable skills for your academic journey, you need to connect your passion, hard work, and educational pursuit to the kinetic powers inside of your mind. Remember, it's OK to take things slow and make errors along the way.

S.W.A.G. TIP #12
Understanding Talent

Most of the talents you possess are a combination of your raw ability and the educational aptitude you acquire.

S.W.A.G. REFLECTION:

What did I learn?

_____

_____

_____

_____

_____

Will I use these tips? (Circle One)   Yes   Maybe   No

Notes:_____

_____

_____

_____

_____

_____

_____

Dream Building

{See YOUR Future, Build YOUR Future}

S.W.A.G. TIP #13

You don't know it all… and because you don't know it all, you need to get a good mentor. All students with academic goals have great mentors.

Mentor Truth 1

Sometimes you have to have people who mentor you and give you that support to make you want to do better. It could be a local business owner, a professor, teacher, or counselor, older uncle, people who have "been there and done that." Mentors who work hard and know what you're going through. They have done inadequately in classes, they've been knocked down, they've lost a love one before, but they still accomplished their dream, which will help you accomplish your dream.

Mentor Truth 2

YOU have to seek out this person!!! It is true that some great mentors will see potential in you and take you under their wings, however most times YOU have to go find the person that can help you become better.

Mentor Truth 3

Most great mentors do not roll out the red carpet for you, they do not sugar coat anything, they are direct, honest, but most importantly passionate about seeing you do better.

FINAL ADVICE:
LISTEN CLOSE TO THEM!!!
APPLY THEIR ADVICE!!
DON'T FORGET TO SAY THANK YOU!!!

S.W.A.G. REFLECTION:

What did I learn?

_____

_____

_____

_____

_____

Will I use these tips? (Circle One)   Yes   Maybe   No

Notes:_____

_____

_____

_____

_____

_____

_____

_____

S.W.A.G. TIP #14
To learn , TEACH

When you study it you remember it, when you teach it you never forget it.

S.W.A.G. TIP #15
You can't stop your thoughts but you don't have to listen to them either.

For starters, accept the fact that your mind will wonder every day and night for the rest of your life. Now that you have accepted that, understand that you control what you do with those thoughts. Some thoughts encourage positive behavior; others may encourage negative behavior. However you and you alone are in control of your thoughts. Remember this, just because you thought it, does not mean you have to do it.

S.W.A.G. REFLECTION:

What did I learn?

_____

_____

_____

_____

_____

Will I use these tips? (Circle One)　　Yes　　Maybe　　No

Notes:_____

_____

_____

_____

_____

_____

_____

S.W.A.G. TIP #16
You get MORE of whatever you focus on

If you want to become a better person, concentrate and focus all of your energy on becoming that.

If you want to become the S.W.A.G. than focus on becoming the S.W.A.G.

You get what you focus on.

S.W.A.G. TIP #17
Exercise everyday

In order to arrive at the level you want to reach, you have to be in shape mentally and physically. It doesn't matter what you do, however you must exercise. Your body is your temple and you have to take care of it. Every day you have to get out and move around a little bit, clear your mind, and keep your blood flowing.

S.W.A.G. REFLECTION:

What did I learn?

_____

_____

_____

_____

_____

Will I use these tips? (Circle One)   Yes   Maybe   No

Notes: _____

_____

_____

_____

_____

_____

_____

_____

S.W.A.G. TIP #18
Time Management

If it's true that You Only Live Once, then the secret to getting things done in your life is by developing time management. The secret to time management is to list everything that you need to complete and then prioritize them in order of importance. PRIORITIZE. Unimportant things and distracting people can wait.

Say This 3 times: My TIME is NOW. My TIME is NOW. My TIME is NOW.

S.W.A.G. TIP #19
Use technology to better yourself

21st century technology has become a very powerful tool for students to use. Take full advantage of everything that technology has to offer. I do agree that many of the games in app stores or online are very addicting, however to become a better student you have to realize that technology can be used for more than just games. Use technology to research and discover ways to become better. If you happen to play games, play games that challenge you, from numbers to words, to memorization.

S.W.A.G. REFLECTION:

What did I learn?

_____

_____

_____

_____

_____

Will I use these tips? (Circle One)   Yes   Maybe   No

Notes:_____

_____

_____

_____

_____

_____

_____

_____

S.W.A.G. TIP #20
Be grateful

It does not matter where you live or what you have. Always remember someone has it worse than you do.

1. Act on Opportunities

In school you may here about conferences, workshops, etc. Act on them. You never know what opportunity will lead you to your goal.

S.W.A.G. TIP #21
Trust is key

Do you trust yourself?

S.W.A.G. REFLECTION:

What did I learn?

_____

_____

_____

_____

_____

Will I use these tips? (Circle One)   Yes   Maybe   No

Notes:_____

_____

_____

_____

_____

_____

_____

S.W.A.G. TIP #22
Positivity Elevates You

Positivity does not just make a difference in your life, it is the difference. Surround yourself with people who fill your spirit with words of victory. Surround yourself with students who inspire you to do better. Surround your thoughts with positive words.

S.W.A.G. TIP #23
Dream hard. Work harder

It's a beautiful thing to dream, however it's more beautiful when you accomplish your dream. After you dream about success, good grades, being wealthy, and making a difference, GET TO WORK.

S.W.A.G. REFLECTION:

What did I learn?

_____

_____

_____

_____

Will I use these tips? (Circle One)   Yes   Maybe   No

Notes:_____

_____

_____

_____

_____

_____

_____

S.W.A.G. TIP #24
Social Media

Be aware of what you write or post on Social Media Pages, Blogs, or on the internet.

Once you post something, it is out there forever.

S.W.A.G. TIP #25
Take 5

It is very important to take a quick break when you are studying and beginning to feel tired. When that happens take 5!!! Get up, stretch, walk around, get some water, and then get back to working hard. This is a very effective way to stay motivated.

S.W.A.G. REFLECTION:

What did I learn?

_____

_____

_____

_____

_____

Will I use these tips? (Circle One)   Yes   Maybe   No

Notes:_____

_____

_____

_____

_____

_____

_____

IT'S SHOW TIME!!!

It's SHOW TIME!!!

SHOW UP

Often times, half of the battle in life is just showing up. In order to truly become the SWAG you have to SHOW UP for your opportunity. Whether that means Showing up for tutoring, showing up to class early, or showing up to your teachers office for extra help, you have to be willing on SHOWING UP to get the results you want. For example, Have you ever been in a class where a student who raises their hand to ask a question gets teased for asking? Well as funny as it may have been to you, that student SHOWED UP to class prepared to learn and advance. Ponder this question. Does it make sense to SHOW UP to watch others live out their dreams, rather than SHOWING UP for your opportunity?

SHOW OUT

Once you have showed up for your opportunity, its time to show out. Now what do I mean by show OUT? Well it's simple; show how hungry you are to learn and maximize your moment. When I was in school I did not want anyone to work harder than me, so in class I showed out. I answered questions, I asked questions, I did any and everything I could do to better myself. Now throughout the course of history these types of students may be commonly referred to as Teachers pets or arrogant students, but in reality they are showing out for their opportunity. If it is true that we only have one life to live, why not show out?

SHUT DOWN

The final step is to shut down, in other words, shut down the competition. After you show up for your opportunity, then Show out during your opportunity, its time to shut down the competition by leaving your mark. Picture world renown performer and musical icon Beyoncé during a performance. She shows up for her opportunity, she shows out for the crowd, and then she shuts down the stage by leaving her mark on all of her fans. Pretty incredible huh? Now picture if you did that in school, how famous would you become?

S.W.A.G. REFLECTION:

What did I learn?

_____

_____

_____

_____

_____

Will I use these tips? (Circle One)   Yes   Maybe   No

Notes:_____

_____

_____

_____

_____

_____

_____

_____

It's YOUR TURN

4 Turns

Turn On

In order to become successful you have to TURN ON your mind at all times. To become the SWAG you have to be willing on TURNING ON that brain of yours to receive the information that's presented to you. Everything will not always be interesting, but ask yourself is it worth it?

Turn UP!!!

Exactly what it means!!! TURN UP!!! This is your education so why not go as hard as you can? Why not get as much out of this educational journey as you can? Let me ask you one more time, if it's true that we only have one life to live, why not Turn Up? TURN UP and go get what's yours.

Turn OFF

Since the beginning of time, people have been jealous of the success of others. So what I need you to do is TURN OFF the haters. Turn off anyone who doesn't believe in you, turn off those who talk about you, turn off those who just want to bring negative things to your life.

Turn Around

After you have TURNED ON your mind, TURNED UP, and TURNED OFF the naysayers, its time for you to TURN AROUND and pull somebody up with you. The fact remains, we all stand on the shoulders of those who have come before us. Don't be afraid to turn around and pull somebody up with you, to help another student in need.

S.W.A.G. REFLECTION:

What did I learn?

_____

_____

_____

_____

_____

Will I use these tips? (Circle One)   Yes   Maybe   No

Notes:_____

_____

_____

_____

_____

_____

_____

_____

S.W.A.G.

Back in Session

S.W.A.G. TIP #26
Plan to succeed

Without a plan, a dream is nothing more than just an idea. As the old saying goes, if you fail to plan, you plan to fail.

Every day you have to be in pursuit of knowledge.

S.W.A.G. TIP #27
Choose to be great

We all have been blessed with the power to choose. Don't fall victim to lowered expectations by people who don't want to be as successful as you.

Choose to be great.

S.W.A.G. REFLECTION:

What did I learn?

_____

_____

_____

_____

_____

Will I use these tips? (Circle One)   Yes   Maybe   No

Notes:_____

_____

_____

_____

_____

_____

_____

_____

S.W.A.G.TIP #28
Be curious

We all have learned at a very young age that discovery is the reason life is worth living. That applies to your education as well, if you are not curious on how to become a better student you will limit yourself.

S.W.A.G. TIP #29
The Champ is here

Inspiration and motivation has been the defining moment in the lives of some of the world's greatest scholars. Research and find inspiration from millions of students who have gone before you, the students who are still fighting to get better. You are a champion and you will become a student with academic goals.

S.W.A.G. REFLECTION:

What did I learn?

_____

_____

_____

_____

_____

Will I use these tips? (Circle One)   Yes   Maybe   No

Notes:_____

_____

_____

_____

_____

_____

_____

_____

S.W.A.G. TIP #30
No Test No Victory

If making millions was easy, if making A's was easy
everybody would do it. Life's a test, you have to learn
how to survive and you have to learn when to adapt.
Now apply that to the classroom, you have to know
when to survive and how to adapt to the things you
don't want to learn.

S.W.A.G. TIP #31
Truth

If not now then when?
If not you, then who?

S.W.A.G. REFLECTION:

What did I learn?

_____

_____

_____

_____

_____

Will I use these tips? (Circle One)   Yes   Maybe   No

Notes:_____

_____

_____

_____

_____

_____

_____

_____

S.W.A.G. TIP #32
Buyers and Sellers

Buy into education and NEVER sell yourself short

S.W.A.G. TIP #33
Get involved!!!

By getting involved in extracurricular activities, you will expand your network and be able to pull from resources that can benefit you in the future. Remember it's not always what you know, it's who knows you!!!

S.W.A.G. REFLECTION:

What did I learn?

_____

_____

_____

_____

_____

Will I use these tips? (Circle One)   Yes   Maybe   No

Notes:_____

_____

_____

_____

_____

_____

_____

_____

S.W.A.G. TIP #34
Make your dream bigger than yourself

Never underestimate the power of your vision, even when all the odds seem against you. Work towards your vision and watch your dream become your reality.

S.W.A.G. TIP #35
Stand Up or Fall Back

Either stand up for your education or fall for whatever people say. Be SMART, educate yourself and take control of your moment.

S.W.A.G. REFLECTION:

What did I learn?

_____

_____

_____

_____

_____

Will I use these tips? (Circle One)   Yes   Maybe   No

Notes:_____

_____

_____

_____

_____

_____

_____

_____

S.W.A.G. TIP #36
No more EXCUSES

Take 100% responsibility for your life. Everyone has a story to tell, from poverty, abuse, neglect, parents, money, race, you name it, however you cannot fall victim to excuses.

S.W.A.G. TIP #37
Be in charge of your mind

The bottom line is that your current failures and successes are all a result of your thoughts and actions. You have to be in charge of your mind. You have to be in charge of what you feed your brain, from TV, music, video games, friends, movies, and everything else your mind absorbs. What you say and what you do will impact your future.

S.W.A.G. REFLECTION:

What did I learn?

_____

_____

_____

_____

_____

Will I use these tips? (Circle One)   Yes   Maybe   No

Notes:_____

_____

_____

_____

_____

_____

_____

_____

S.W.A.G. TIP #38
Ask Ask Ask

Don't be afraid to ask. Most people are afraid to ask for feedback about how they are doing because they are afraid of what the response may be or that people will make fun of them. Trust me, there is nothing to be afraid of, besides the only way to get better is for people to tell you the truth.

S.W.A.G. TIP #39
Why are you here?

What's your purpose in life? To live out your purpose means that you are doing what you love to do and you are making a difference. To live out your purpose means to be educated because you are attracting all of the resources and opportunities that you desire.

What is your purpose?_____

_____

_____

For example my purpose, is to inspire students around the world to believe in their education

Find your purpose and live in victory…

S.W.A.G. REFLECTION:

What did I learn?

_____

_____

_____

_____

_____

Will I use these tips? (Circle One)   Yes   Maybe   No

Notes:_____

_____

_____

_____

_____

_____

_____

_____

S.W.A.G. TIP #40
Follow your dream not someone else's

It does not matter what other people want or expect for you to be, look inside of your heart and live out your dreams. Students with academic goals understand that true happiness comes from following **THEIR** dreams. Be passionate about what you want to be and GO GET WHAT'S YOURS.

S.W.A.G. TIP #41
Ignore Negative People

Don't let anyone talk you out of your vision. To become the S.W.A.G. don't let dream killers, destroy what you want to be. With hard work and dedication YOU CAN become whatever you want to be. Now it is true, we all can't become professional athletes, celebrities, or famous rock stars, but we all can become successful. Always remember you are wonderfully made and created for greatness.

S.W.A.G. REFLECTION:

What did I learn?

_____

_____

_____

_____

_____

Will I use these tips? (Circle One)   Yes   Maybe   No

Notes:_____

_____

_____

_____

_____

_____

_____

_____

S.W.A.G. TIP #42
Believe in yourself

Believing in you is a choice. Listen it is unfortunate if you do not have the resources for you to follow your dreams; however that should never stop you from believing in yourself. You and ONLY YOU have to take control of your dreams.

S.W.A.G. TIP #43
Stop saying I Can't

If you are going to be successful, you need to give up the phrase I can't. I can't makes you powerless and allows fear to sneak inside of your mind.

Say this 3 times

I can't is for those who are scared. I can't is for those who are scared. I can't is for those who are scared.

S.W.A.G. REFLECTION:

What did I learn?

_____

_____

_____

_____

_____

Will I use these tips? (Circle One)   Yes   Maybe   No

Notes:_____

_____

_____

_____

_____

_____

_____

_____

S.W.A.G. TIP #44
Positive Strides

During each day you are faced with a choice: You can either focus your attention on what you want to accomplish or you can entertain the possibility of making a mistake. Remember making errors are normal, learn from them and keep going.

S.W.A.G. TIP #45
Do it NOW!!!

One of the most famous companies in the world has made a fortune off of this principle. Listen to me, whatever you want to become, whatever you have to do to get the grade you want, DO IT NOW!!!

S.W.A.G. REFLECTION:

What did I learn?

_____

_____

_____

_____

_____

Will I use these tips? (Circle One)   Yes   Maybe   No

Notes:_____

_____

_____

_____

_____

_____

_____

_____

_____

S.W.A.G. TIP #46
Say goodbye to your comfort zones

Think of your comfort zone as a prison you create for yourself that limits everything you are capable of. You have to come out of your comfort zone, even if that means walking alone.

Do not limit yourself

S.W.A.G. TIP #47
Paint your own picture

Stop waiting for motivation or for someone to come along and do it for you, paint your picture and live it every single day.

S.W.A.G. REFLECTION:

What did I learn?

_____

_____

_____

_____

_____

Will I use these tips? (Circle One)   Yes   Maybe   No

Notes:_____

_____

_____

_____

_____

_____

_____

_____

S.W.A.G.TIP #48
Pay the PRICE

Don't let society fool you, behind every big achievement is a story of education, hard work, hours of practice, discipline, and personal sacrifice. It does not matter how frightening it may be, you have to be willing to pay the price for success. You may have to tell your friends you can't have fun right now because you have homework, or you may have to skip the movies to work an extra hour on your paper, no matter what it is I can promise you if you are willing on paying the price you will do well.

S.W.A.G. TIP #49
Put in WORK

If you want something bad enough, you have to put in work. Part of paying the price to become the S.W.A.G. is your enthusiasm to do whatever it takes to get the required job done. It comes from a strong personal commitment to get it done no matter what it takes, how long it takes, or what distractions may come your way. Put your priorities in check. At the end of the day you are responsible for the results you desire.

S.W.A.G. TIP #50
Slow progress is still progress!!!

Listen to me SLOW PROGRESS is STILL PROGRESS. If you go from a C to a B that's progress, entry-level to mid-manager that's progress, even if you don't get into a leadership development program or land that dream job right away, but get hired somewhere that's progress, so celebrate that progress. Listen, we all don't move as fast as others, however as long as you are moving forward in a positive productive direction, you are doing great.

S.W.A.G. REFLECTION:

What did I learn?

_____

_____

_____

_____

_____

Will I use these tips? (Circle One)   Yes   Maybe   No

Notes:_____

_____

_____

_____

_____

_____

_____

_____

S.W.A.G.

Bonus Tips

I've provided you with two additional tips, to represent going beyond what's expected of you. If your teacher or professor requires you to do 5 homework problems, do 10. Take the initiative to go further than most students would go.

S.W.A.G. TIP #51
Every promise you make is with yourself

No matter what you do in life, you are ultimately making promises and commitments with yourself. You have to be honest with yourself every day and you have to understand that if you say you are going to do something, you have to do it. If you do not, you are subconsciously building a bad habit to distrust yourself.

S.W.A.G. TIP #52
Mirror Check

Every day walk in front of a mirror and tell yourself positive things. Say to yourself, I'm So Educated™, I CAN DO IT, I plan to achieve great things today, anything positive. If you have to, get post it notes and post positive things you want to achieve on your mirror and look at yourself as you read them to yourself.

Before bed, perform a mirror check and ask yourself have you lied to yourself.

S.W.A.G. REFLECTION:

What did I learn?

_____

_____

_____

_____

_____

Will I use these tips? (Circle One)   Yes   Maybe   No

Notes:_____

_____

_____

_____

_____

_____

_____

_____

NETWORKING

Networking

There is a phrase out there that says "Expand your Network, and you will increase your Net Worth.

Take a second and think about this question.

How do you Network???

Remember these 10 key tips:

1. Networking is not about Quantity it's about QUALITY!!!
   We are all one person from where we want to be in life.
2. Introduce yourself, Ask Questions, Smile
3. Always be Prepared (Research those that you can)
4. Have your elevator pitch ready. (Who you are, What skills you have, Why that's important)
5. Practice talking in the mirror with friends, and strangers. (Practice helps)
6. Don't be afraid of the power players!!! Remember you're human just like any CEO, Executive, or Hiring Manager
7. Take advantage of social media, and leverage that by building meaningful relationships.
8. Networking is not always about what someone can do for you, it is about what you can do for them.
9. Listen more than you talk. (There is great value from learning about the experiences of people)
10. Be Authentic

S.W.A.G.

Productive Checklist

30 Day Jump Start

S.W.A.G. Checklist
Each day as you complete something circle it.
(30 Day Jump Start)

DAY 1

Studied

Reviewed notes

Read ahead

Created goals for tomorrow

Updated my calendar

Completed my Homework

Watched the news

Wrote in my journal

Complete any projects

Sent out any Thank You cards

Organized my notes

Exercised

Searched for Jobs

Searched for Scholarships

Made any appointments

Read news articles (Local, National, International)

Tried something new

5 minute break

Looked at my study guide

Talked to my mentor

Created questions to ask in class tomorrow

Selected clothes for tomorrow

Looked at my dream building section

Reviewed my goals

Updated my LinkedIn page

What did I not accomplish that I wanted to?_____

_____

Goals for tomorrow?_____

S.W.A.G. Checklist
Each day as you complete something scratch it off.
(30 Day Jump Start)

DAY 2

Studied

Reviewed notes

Read ahead

Created goals for tomorrow

Updated my calendar

Completed my Homework

Watched the news

Wrote in my journal

Complete any projects

Sent out any Thank You cards

Organized my notes

Exercised

Searched for Jobs

Searched for Scholarships

Made any appointments

Read news articles (Local, National, International)

Tried something new

5 minute break

Looked at my study guide

Talked to my mentor

Created questions to ask in class tomorrow

Selected clothes for tomorrow

Looked at my dream building section

Reviewed my goals

Updated my LinkedIn page

What did I not accomplish that I wanted to?_____

_____

Goals for tomorrow?_____

S.W.A.G. Checklist
Each day as you complete something circle it.
(30 Day Jump Start)

DAY 3

Studied

Reviewed notes

Read ahead

Created goals for tomorrow

Updated my calendar

Completed my Homework

Watched the news

Wrote in my journal

Complete any projects

Sent out any Thank You cards

Organized my notes

Exercised

Searched for Jobs

Searched for Scholarships

Made any appointments

Read news articles (Local, National, International)

Tried something new

5 minute break

Looked at my study guide

Talked to my mentor

Created questions to ask in class tomorrow

Selected clothes for tomorrow

Looked at my dream building section

Reviewed my goals

Updated my LinkedIn page

What did I not accomplish that I wanted to?_____

_____

Goals for tomorrow?_____

S.W.A.G. Checklist
Each day as you complete something circle it.
(30 Day Jump Start)

DAY 4

Studied

Reviewed notes

Read ahead

Created goals for tomorrow

Updated my calendar

Completed my Homework

Watched the news

Wrote in my journal

Complete any projects

Sent out any Thank You cards

Organized my notes

Exercised

Searched for Jobs

Searched for Scholarships

Made any appointments

Read news articles (Local, National, International)

Tried something new

5 minute break

Looked at my study guide

Talked to my mentor

Created questions to ask in class tomorrow

Selected clothes for tomorrow

Looked at my dream building section

Reviewed my goals

Updated my LinkedIn page

What did I not accomplish that I wanted to?_____

_____

Goals for tomorrow?_____

S.W.A.G. Checklist
**Each day as you complete something circle it.
(30 Day Jump Start)**

DAY 5

Studied

Reviewed notes

Read ahead

Created goals for tomorrow

Updated my calendar

Completed my Homework

Watched the news

Wrote in my journal

Complete any projects

Sent out any Thank You cards

Organized my notes

Exercised

Searched for Jobs

Searched for Scholarships

Made any appointments

Read news articles (Local, National, International)

Tried something new

5 minute break

Looked at my study guide

Talked to my mentor

Created questions to ask in class tomorrow

Selected clothes for tomorrow

Looked at my dream building section

Reviewed my goals

Updated my LinkedIn page

What did I not accomplish that I wanted to?_____

_____

Goals for tomorrow?_____

S.W.A.G. Checklist
**Each day as you complete something circle it.
(30 Day Jump Start)**

DAY 6

Studied

Reviewed notes

Read ahead

Created goals for tomorrow

Updated my calendar

Completed my Homework

Watched the news

Wrote in my journal

Complete any projects

Sent out any Thank You cards

Organized my notes

Exercised

Searched for Jobs

Searched for Scholarships

Made any appointments

Read news articles (Local, National, International)

Tried something new

5 minute break

Looked at my study guide

Talked to my mentor

Created questions to ask in class tomorrow

Selected clothes for tomorrow

Looked at my dream building section

Reviewed my goals

Updated my LinkedIn page

What did I not accomplish that I wanted to?_____

_____

Goals for tomorrow?_____

S.W.A.G. Checklist
Each day as you complete something circle it.
(30 Day Jump Start)

DAY 7

Studied

Reviewed notes

Read ahead

Created goals for tomorrow

Updated my calendar

Completed my Homework

Watched the news

Wrote in my journal

Complete any projects

Sent out any Thank You cards

Organized my notes

Exercised

Searched for Jobs

Searched for Scholarships

Made any appointments

Read news articles (Local, National, International)

Tried something new

5 minute break

Looked at my study guide

Talked to my mentor

Created questions to ask in class tomorrow

Selected clothes for tomorrow

Looked at my dream building section

Reviewed my goals

Updated my LinkedIn page

What did I not accomplish that I wanted to?_____

_____

Goals for tomorrow?_____

S.W.A.G. Checklist
Each day as you complete something circle it.
(30 Day Jump Start)

DAY 8

Studied

Reviewed notes

Read ahead

Created goals for tomorrow

Updated my calendar

Completed my Homework

Watched the news

Wrote in my journal

Complete any projects

Sent out any Thank You cards

Organized my notes

Exercised

Searched for Jobs

Searched for Scholarships

Made any appointments

Read news articles (Local, National, International)

Tried something new

5 minute break

Looked at my study guide

Talked to my mentor

Created questions to ask in class tomorrow

Selected clothes for tomorrow

Looked at my dream building section

Reviewed my goals

Updated my LinkedIn page

What did I not accomplish that I wanted to?_____

_____

Goals for tomorrow?_____

S.W.A.G. Checklist
Each day as you complete something circle it.
(30 Day Jump Start)

DAY 9

Studied

Reviewed notes

Read ahead

Created goals for tomorrow

Updated my calendar

Completed my Homework

Watched the news

Wrote in my journal

Complete any projects

Sent out any Thank You cards

Organized my notes

Exercised

Searched for Jobs

Searched for Scholarships

Made any appointments

Read news articles (Local, National, International)

Tried something new

5 minute break

Looked at my study guide

Talked to my mentor

Created questions to ask in class tomorrow

Selected clothes for tomorrow

Looked at my dream building section

Reviewed my goals

Updated my LinkedIn page

What did I not accomplish that I wanted to?_____

_____

Goals for tomorrow?_____

S.W.A.G. Checklist
Each day as you complete something circle it.
(30 Day Jump Start)

DAY 10

Studied

Reviewed notes

Read ahead

Created goals for tomorrow

Updated my calendar

Completed my Homework

Watched the news

Wrote in my journal

Complete any projects

Sent out any Thank You cards

Organized my notes

Exercised

Searched for Jobs

Searched for Scholarships

Made any appointments

Read news articles (Local, National, International)

Tried something new

5 minute break

Looked at my study guide

Talked to my mentor

Created questions to ask in class tomorrow

Selected clothes for tomorrow

Looked at my dream building section

Reviewed my goals

Updated my LinkedIn page

What did I not accomplish that I wanted to?_____

_____

Goals for tomorrow?_____

S.W.A.G. Checklist
Each day as you complete something circle it.
(30 Day Jump Start)

DAY 11

Studied

Reviewed notes

Read ahead

Created goals for tomorrow

Updated my calendar

Completed my Homework

Watched the news

Wrote in my journal

Complete any projects

Sent out any Thank You cards

Organized my notes

Exercised

Searched for Jobs

Searched for Scholarships

Made any appointments

Read news articles (Local, National, International)

Tried something new

5 minute break

Looked at my study guide

Talked to my mentor

Created questions to ask in class tomorrow

Selected clothes for tomorrow

Looked at my dream building section

Reviewed my goals

Updated my LinkedIn page

What did I not accomplish that I wanted to?_____

_____

Goals for tomorrow?_____

S.W.A.G. Checklist
Each day as you complete something circle it.
(30 Day Jump Start)

DAY 12

Studied

Reviewed notes

Read ahead

Created goals for tomorrow

Updated my calendar

Completed my Homework

Watched the news

Wrote in my journal

Complete any projects

Sent out any Thank You cards

Organized my notes

Exercised

Searched for Jobs

Searched for Scholarships

Made any appointments

Read news articles (Local, National, International)

Tried something new

5 minute break

Looked at my study guide

Talked to my mentor

Created questions to ask in class tomorrow

Selected clothes for tomorrow

Looked at my dream building section

Reviewed my goals

Updated my LinkedIn page

What did I not accomplish that I wanted to?_____

_____

Goals for tomorrow?_____

S.W.A.G. Checklist
Each day as you complete something circle it.
(30 Day Jump Start)

DAY 13

Studied

Reviewed notes

Read ahead

Created goals for tomorrow

Updated my calendar

Completed my Homework

Watched the news

Wrote in my journal

Complete any projects

Sent out any Thank You cards

Organized my notes

Exercised

Searched for Jobs

Searched for Scholarships

Made any appointments

Read news articles (Local, National, International)

Tried something new

5 minute break

Looked at my study guide

Talked to my mentor

Created questions to ask in class tomorrow

Selected clothes for tomorrow

Looked at my dream building section

Reviewed my goals

Updated my LinkedIn page

What did I not accomplish that I wanted to?_____

_____

Goals for tomorrow?_____

S.W.A.G. Checklist
Each day as you complete something circle it.
(30 Day Jump Start)

DAY 14

Studied

Reviewed notes

Read ahead

Created goals for tomorrow

Updated my calendar

Completed my Homework

Watched the news

Wrote in my journal

Complete any projects

Sent out any Thank You cards

Organized my notes

Exercised

Searched for Jobs

Searched for Scholarships

Made any appointments

Read news articles (Local, National, International)

Tried something new

5 minute break

Looked at my study guide

Talked to my mentor

Created questions to ask in class tomorrow

Selected clothes for tomorrow

Looked at my dream building section

Reviewed my goals

Updated my LinkedIn page

What did I not accomplish that I wanted to?_____

_____

Goals for tomorrow?_____

S.W.A.G. Checklist
Each day as you complete something circle it.
(30 Day Jump Start)

DAY 15

Studied

Reviewed notes

Read ahead

Created goals for tomorrow

Updated my calendar

Completed my Homework

Watched the news

Wrote in my journal

Complete any projects

Sent out any Thank You cards

Organized my notes

Exercised

Searched for Jobs

Searched for Scholarships

Made any appointments

Read news articles (Local, National, International)

Tried something new

5 minute break

Looked at my study guide

Talked to my mentor

Created questions to ask in class tomorrow

Selected clothes for tomorrow

Looked at my dream building section

Reviewed my goals

Updated my LinkedIn page

What did I not accomplish that I wanted to?_____

_____

Goals for tomorrow?_____

S.W.A.G. Checklist
Each day as you complete something circle it.
(30 Day Jump Start)

DAY 16

Studied

Reviewed notes

Read ahead

Created goals for tomorrow

Updated my calendar

Completed my Homework

Watched the news

Wrote in my journal

Complete any projects

Sent out any Thank You cards

Organized my notes

Exercised

Searched for Jobs

Searched for Scholarships

Made any appointments

Read news articles (Local, National, International)

Tried something new

5 minute break

Looked at my study guide

Talked to my mentor

Created questions to ask in class tomorrow

Selected clothes for tomorrow

Looked at my dream building section

Reviewed my goals

Updated my LinkedIn page

What did I not accomplish that I wanted to?_____

_____

Goals for tomorrow?_____

S.W.A.G. Checklist
Each day as you complete something circle it.
(30 Day Jump Start)

DAY 17

Studied

Reviewed notes

Read ahead

Created goals for tomorrow

Updated my calendar

Completed my Homework

Watched the news

Wrote in my journal

Complete any projects

Sent out any Thank You cards

Organized my notes

Exercised

Searched for Jobs

Searched for Scholarships

Made any appointments

Read news articles (Local, National, International)

Tried something new

5 minute break

Looked at my study guide

Talked to my mentor

Created questions to ask in class tomorrow

Selected clothes for tomorrow

Looked at my dream building section

Reviewed my goals

Updated my LinkedIn page

What did I not accomplish that I wanted to?_____

_____

Goals for tomorrow?_____

S.W.A.G. Checklist
Each day as you complete something circle it.
(30 Day Jump Start)

DAY 18

Studied

Reviewed notes

Read ahead

Created goals for tomorrow

Updated my calendar

Completed my Homework

Watched the news

Wrote in my journal

Complete any projects

Sent out any Thank You cards

Organized my notes

Exercised

Searched for Jobs

Searched for Scholarships

Made any appointments

Read news articles (Local, National, International)

Tried something new

5 minute break

Looked at my study guide

Talked to my mentor

Created questions to ask in class tomorrow

Selected clothes for tomorrow

Looked at my dream building section

Reviewed my goals

Updated my LinkedIn page

What did I not accomplish that I wanted to?_____

_____

Goals for tomorrow?_____

S.W.A.G. Checklist
Each day as you complete something circle it.
(30 Day Jump Start)

DAY 19

Studied

Reviewed notes

Read ahead

Created goals for tomorrow

Updated my calendar

Completed my Homework

Watched the news

Wrote in my journal

Complete any projects

Sent out any Thank You cards

Organized my notes

Exercised

Searched for Jobs

Searched for Scholarships

Made any appointments

Read news articles (Local, National, International)

Tried something new

5 minute break

Looked at my study guide

Talked to my mentor

Created questions to ask in class tomorrow

Selected clothes for tomorrow

Looked at my dream building section

Reviewed my goals

Updated my LinkedIn page

What did I not accomplish that I wanted to?_____

_____

Goals for tomorrow?_____

S.W.A.G. Checklist
Each day as you complete something circle it.
(30 Day Jump Start)

DAY 20

Studied

Reviewed notes

Read ahead

Created goals for tomorrow

Updated my calendar

Completed my Homework

Watched the news

Wrote in my journal

Complete any projects

Sent out any Thank You cards

Organized my notes

Exercised

Searched for Jobs

Searched for Scholarships

Made any appointments

Read news articles (Local, National, International)

Tried something new

5 minute break

Looked at my study guide

Talked to my mentor

Created questions to ask in class tomorrow

Selected clothes for tomorrow

Looked at my dream building section

Reviewed my goals

Updated my LinkedIn page

What did I not accomplish that I wanted to?_____

_____

Goals for tomorrow?_____

S.W.A.G. Checklist
Each day as you complete something circle it.
(30 Day Jump Start)

DAY 21

Studied

Reviewed notes

Read ahead

Created goals for tomorrow

Updated my calendar

Completed my Homework

Watched the news

Wrote in my journal

Complete any projects

Sent out any Thank You cards

Organized my notes

Exercised

Searched for Jobs

Searched for Scholarships

Made any appointments

Read news articles (Local, National, International)

Tried something new

5 minute break

Looked at my study guide

Talked to my mentor

Created questions to ask in class tomorrow

Selected clothes for tomorrow

Looked at my dream building section

Reviewed my goals

Updated my LinkedIn page

What did I not accomplish that I wanted to?_____

_____

Goals for tomorrow?_____

S.W.A.G. Checklist
Each day as you complete something circle it.
(30 Day Jump Start)

DAY 22

Studied

Reviewed notes

Read ahead

Created goals for tomorrow

Updated my calendar

Completed my Homework

Watched the news

Wrote in my journal

Complete any projects

Sent out any Thank You cards

Organized my notes

Exercised

Searched for Jobs

Searched for Scholarships

Made any appointments

Read news articles (Local, National, International)

Tried something new

5 minute break

Looked at my study guide

Talked to my mentor

Created questions to ask in class tomorrow

Selected clothes for tomorrow

Looked at my dream building section

Reviewed my goals

Updated my LinkedIn page

What did I not accomplish that I wanted to?_____

_____

Goals for tomorrow?_____

S.W.A.G. Checklist
Each day as you complete something circle it.
(30 Day Jump Start)

DAY 23

Studied

Reviewed notes

Read ahead

Created goals for tomorrow

Updated my calendar

Completed my Homework

Watched the news

Wrote in my journal

Complete any projects

Sent out any Thank You cards

Organized my notes

Exercised

Searched for Jobs

Searched for Scholarships

Made any appointments

Read news articles (Local, National, International)

Tried something new

5 minute break

Looked at my study guide

Talked to my mentor

Created questions to ask in class tomorrow

Selected clothes for tomorrow

Looked at my dream building section

Reviewed my goals

Updated my LinkedIn page

What did I not accomplish that I wanted to?_____

_____   _____

Goals for tomorrow?_____

S.W.A.G. Checklist
Each day as you complete something circle it.
(30 Day Jump Start)

DAY 24

Studied

Reviewed notes

Read ahead

Created goals for tomorrow

Updated my calendar

Completed my Homework

Watched the news

Wrote in my journal

Complete any projects

Sent out any Thank You cards

Organized my notes

Exercised

Searched for Jobs

Searched for Scholarships

Made any appointments

Read news articles (Local, National, International)

Tried something new

5 minute break

Looked at my study guide

Talked to my mentor

Created questions to ask in class tomorrow

Selected clothes for tomorrow

Looked at my dream building section

Reviewed my goals

Updated my LinkedIn page

What did I not accomplish that I wanted to?_____

_____

Goals for tomorrow?_____

S.W.A.G. Checklist
Each day as you complete something circle it.
(30 Day Jump Start)

DAY 25

Studied

Reviewed notes

Read ahead

Created goals for tomorrow

Updated my calendar

Completed my Homework

Watched the news

Wrote in my journal

Complete any projects

Sent out any Thank You cards

Organized my notes

Exercised

Searched for Jobs

Searched for Scholarships

Made any appointments

Read news articles (Local, National, International)

Tried something new

5 minute break

Looked at my study guide

Talked to my mentor

Created questions to ask in class tomorrow

Selected clothes for tomorrow

Looked at my dream building section

Reviewed my goals

Updated my LinkedIn page

What did I not accomplish that I wanted to?_____

_____

Goals for tomorrow?_____

S.W.A.G. Checklist
Each day as you complete something circle it.
(30 Day Jump Start)

DAY 26

Studied

Reviewed notes

Read ahead

Created goals for tomorrow

Updated my calendar

Completed my Homework

Watched the news

Wrote in my journal

Complete any projects

Sent out any Thank You cards

Organized my notes

Exercised

Searched for Jobs

Searched for Scholarships

Made any appointments

Read news articles (Local, National, International)

Tried something new

5 minute break

Looked at my study guide

Talked to my mentor

Created questions to ask in class tomorrow

Selected clothes for tomorrow

Looked at my dream building section

Reviewed my goals

Updated my LinkedIn page

What did I not accomplish that I wanted to?_____

_____

Goals for tomorrow?_____

S.W.A.G. Checklist
Each day as you complete something circle it.
(30 Day Jump Start)

DAY 27

Studied

Reviewed notes

Read ahead

Created goals for tomorrow

Updated my calendar

Completed my Homework

Watched the news

Wrote in my journal

Complete any projects

Sent out any Thank You cards

Organized my notes

Exercised

Searched for Jobs

Searched for Scholarships

Made any appointments

Read news articles (Local, National, International)

Tried something new

5 minute break

Looked at my study guide

Talked to my mentor

Created questions to ask in class tomorrow

Selected clothes for tomorrow

Looked at my dream building section

Reviewed my goals

Updated my LinkedIn page

What did I not accomplish that I wanted to?_____

_____

Goals for tomorrow?_____

S.W.A.G. Checklist
Each day as you complete something circle it.
(30 Day Jump Start)

DAY 28

Studied

Reviewed notes

Read ahead

Created goals for tomorrow

Updated my calendar

Completed my Homework

Watched the news

Wrote in my journal

Complete any projects

Sent out any Thank You cards

Organized my notes

Exercised

Searched for Jobs

Searched for Scholarships

Made any appointments

Read news articles (Local, National, International)

Tried something new

5 minute break

Looked at my study guide

Talked to my mentor

Created questions to ask in class tomorrow

Selected clothes for tomorrow

Looked at my dream building section

Reviewed my goals

Updated my LinkedIn page

What did I not accomplish that I wanted to?_____

_____

Goals for tomorrow?_____

S.W.A.G. Checklist
Each day as you complete something circle it.
(30 Day Jump Start)

DAY 29

Studied

Reviewed notes

Read ahead

Created goals for tomorrow

Updated my calendar

Completed my Homework

Watched the news

Wrote in my journal

Complete any projects

Sent out any Thank You cards

Organized my notes

Exercised

Searched for Jobs

Searched for Scholarships

Made any appointments

Read news articles (Local, National, International)

Tried something new

5 minute break

Looked at my study guide

Talked to my mentor

Created questions to ask in class tomorrow

Selected clothes for tomorrow

Looked at my dream building section

Reviewed my goals

Updated my LinkedIn page

What did I not accomplish that I wanted to?_____

_____

Goals for tomorrow?_____

S.W.A.G. Checklist
Each day as you complete something circle it.
(30 Day Jump Start)

DAY 30

Studied

Reviewed notes

Read ahead

Created goals for tomorrow

Updated my calendar

Completed my Homework

Watched the news

Wrote in my journal

Complete any projects

Sent out any Thank You cards

Organized my notes

Exercised

Searched for Jobs

Searched for Scholarships

Made any appointments

Read news articles (Local, National, International)

Tried something new

5 minute break

Looked at my study guide

Talked to my mentor

Created questions to ask in class tomorrow

Selected clothes for tomorrow

Looked at my dream building section

Reviewed my goals

Updated my LinkedIn page

What did I not accomplish that I wanted to?_____

_____

Goals for tomorrow?_____

GOAL-SETTING WORKSHEETS

30 Day Jump Start

Students With Academic Goals
(30 Day jump Start Goal Worksheet)

Day 1

What do you want to
accomplish?_____
(Be Specific)

When do you want to complete it?_____

Why is completing this goal
important?_____

What Steps do you have to take to reach your goal?(Think
about how many steps you need)
1.
2.
3.
4.
5.

What obstacles or distractions do you think will prevent you
from reaching this goal?(including
friends)_____

How will you deal with these obstacles in order to achieve your
goal?

How will you measure your success and track your progress?
(daily or weekly)_____

Did you accomplish your goal?

Yes   Work in Progress   No

Students With Academic Goals
(30 Day jump Start Goal Worksheet)

Day 2

What do you want to
accomplish?_____
(Be Specific)

When do you want to complete it?_____

Why is completing this goal
important?   _____

What Steps do you have to take to reach your goal?(Think
about how many steps you need)
1.
2.
3.
4.
5.

What obstacles or distractions do you think will prevent you
from reaching this goal?(including
friends)_____

How will you deal with these obstacles in order to achieve your
goal?

How will you measure your success and track your progress?
(daily or weekly)_____

Did you accomplish your goal?

Yes   Work in Progress   No

Students With Academic Goals
(30 Day jump Start Goal Worksheet)

Day 3

What do you want to
accomplish?_____
(Be Specific)

When do you want to complete it?_____

Why is completing this goal
important?_____

What Steps do you have to take to reach your goal?(Think
about how many steps you need)
1.
2.
3.
4.
5.

What obstacles or distractions do you think will prevent you
from reaching this goal?(including
friends)_____

How will you deal with these obstacles in order to achieve your
goal?

How will you measure your success and track your progress?
(daily or weekly)_____

Did you accomplish your goal?

Yes   Work in Progress   No

Students With Academic Goals
(30 Day jump Start Goal Worksheet)

Day 4

What do you want to
accomplish?_____
(Be Specific)

When do you want to complete it?_____

Why is completing this goal
important?_____   _____

What Steps do you have to take to reach your goal?(Think
about how many steps you need)
1.
2.
3.
4.
5.

What obstacles or distractions do you think will prevent you
from reaching this goal?(including
friends)_____   _____

How will you deal with these obstacles in order to achieve your
goal?

How will you measure your success and track your progress?
(daily or weekly)_____

Did you accomplish your goal?

Yes   Work in Progress   No

Students With Academic Goals
(30 Day jump Start Goal Worksheet)

Day 5

What do you want to
accomplish?_____
(Be Specific)

When do you want to complete it?_____

Why is completing this goal
important?_____

What Steps do you have to take to reach your goal?(Think
about how many steps you need)
1.
2.
3.
4.
5.

What obstacles or distractions do you think will prevent you
from reaching this goal?(including
friends)_____

How will you deal with these obstacles in order to achieve your
goal?

How will you measure your success and track your progress?
(daily or weekly)_____

Did you accomplish your goal?

Yes   Work in Progress   No

Students With Academic Goals
(30 Day jump Start Goal Worksheet)

Day 6

What do you want to
accomplish?_____
(Be Specific)

When do you want to complete it?_____

Why is completing this goal
important?_____

What Steps do you have to take to reach your goal?(Think
about how many steps you need)
1.
2.
3.
4.
5.

What obstacles or distractions do you think will prevent you
from reaching this goal?(including
friends)_____ _____

How will you deal with these obstacles in order to achieve your
goal?

How will you measure your success and track your progress?
(daily or weekly)_____

Did you accomplish your goal?

Yes   Work in Progress   No

Students With Academic Goals
(30 Day jump Start Goal Worksheet)

Day 7

What do you want to
accomplish?_____
(Be Specific)

When do you want to complete it?_____

Why is completing this goal
important?_____

What Steps do you have to take to reach your goal?(Think
about how many steps you need)
1.
2.
3.
4.
5.

What obstacles or distractions do you think will prevent you
from reaching this goal?(including
friends)_____

How will you deal with these obstacles in order to achieve your
goal?

How will you measure your success and track your progress?
(daily or weekly)_____

Did you accomplish your goal?

Yes   Work in Progress   No

Students With Academic Goals
(30 Day jump Start Goal Worksheet)

Day 8

What do you want to
accomplish?_____
(Be Specific)

When do you want to complete it?_____

Why is completing this goal
important? _____   _____

What Steps do you have to take to reach your goal?(Think
about how many steps you need)
1.
2.
3.
4.
5.

What obstacles or distractions do you think will prevent you
from reaching this goal?(including
friends)_____

How will you deal with these obstacles in order to achieve your
goal?

How will you measure your success and track your progress?
(daily or weekly)_____

Did you accomplish your goal?

Yes   Work in Progress   No

Students With Academic Goals
(30 Day jump Start Goal Worksheet)

Day 9

What do you want to
accomplish?_____
(Be Specific)

When do you want to complete it?_____

Why is completing this goal
important?_____

What Steps do you have to take to reach your goal?(Think
about how many steps you need)
1.
2.
3.
4.
5.

What obstacles or distractions do you think will prevent you
from reaching this goal?(including
friends)_____

How will you deal with these obstacles in order to achieve your
goal?

How will you measure your success and track your progress?
(daily or weekly)_____

Did you accomplish your goal?

Yes   Work in Progress   No

Students With Academic Goals
(30 Day jump Start Goal Worksheet)

Day 10

What do you want to
accomplish?_____
(Be Specific)

When do you want to complete it?_____

Why is completing this goal
important?_____

What Steps do you have to take to reach your goal?(Think
about how many steps you need)
1.
2.
3.
4.
5.

What obstacles or distractions do you think will prevent you
from reaching this goal?(including
friends)_____

How will you deal with these obstacles in order to achieve your
goal?

How will you measure your success and track your progress?
(daily or weekly)_____

Did you accomplish your goal?

Yes   Work in Progress   No

Students With Academic Goals
(30 Day jump Start Goal Worksheet)

Day 11

What do you want to
accomplish?_____
(Be Specific)

When do you want to complete it?_____

Why is completing this goal
important?_____

What Steps do you have to take to reach your goal?(Think
about how many steps you need)
1.
2.
3.
4.
5.

What obstacles or distractions do you think will prevent you
from reaching this goal?(including
friends)_____

How will you deal with these obstacles in order to achieve your
goal?

How will you measure your success and track your progress?
(daily or weekly)_____

Did you accomplish your goal?

Yes   Work in Progress   No

Students With Academic Goals
(30 Day jump Start Goal Worksheet)

Day 12

What do you want to
accomplish?_____
(Be Specific)

When do you want to complete it?_____

Why is completing this goal
important?_____   _____

What Steps do you have to take to reach your goal?(Think
about how many steps you need)
1.
2.
3.
4.
5.

What obstacles or distractions do you think will prevent you
from reaching this goal?(including
friends)_____

How will you deal with these obstacles in order to achieve your
goal?

How will you measure your success and track your progress?
(daily or weekly)_____

Did you accomplish your goal?

Yes   Work in Progress   No

Students With Academic Goals
(30 Day jump Start Goal Worksheet)

Day 13

What do you want to
accomplish?_____
(Be Specific)

When do you want to complete it?_____

Why is completing this goal
important?_____

What Steps do you have to take to reach your goal?(Think
about how many steps you need)
1.
2.
3.
4.
5.

What obstacles or distractions do you think will prevent you
from reaching this goal?(including
friends)_____

How will you deal with these obstacles in order to achieve your
goal?

How will you measure your success and track your progress?
(daily or weekly)_____

Did you accomplish your goal?

Yes   Work in Progress   No

Students With Academic Goals
(30 Day jump Start Goal Worksheet)

Day 14

What do you want to
accomplish?_____
(Be Specific)

When do you want to complete it?_____

Why is completing this goal
important?_____

What Steps do you have to take to reach your goal?(Think
about how many steps you need)
1.
2.
3.
4.
5.

What obstacles or distractions do you think will prevent you
from reaching this goal?(including
friends)____ _____

How will you deal with these obstacles in order to achieve your
goal?

How will you measure your success and track your progress?
(daily or weekly)_____

Did you accomplish your goal?

Yes   Work in Progress   No

Students With Academic Goals
(30 Day jump Start Goal Worksheet)

Day 15

What do you want to
accomplish?_____
(Be Specific)

When do you want to complete it?_____

Why is completing this goal
important?_____

What Steps do you have to take to reach your goal?(Think
about how many steps you need)
1.
2.
3.
4.
5.

What obstacles or distractions do you think will prevent you
from reaching this goal?(including
friends)_____

How will you deal with these obstacles in order to achieve your
goal?

How will you measure your success and track your progress?
(daily or weekly)_____

Did you accomplish your goal?

Yes   Work in Progress   No

Students With Academic Goals
(30 Day jump Start Goal Worksheet)

Day 16

What do you want to
accomplish?_____
(Be Specific)

When do you want to complete it?_____

Why is completing this goal
important?_____   _____

What Steps do you have to take to reach your goal?(Think
about how many steps you need)
1.
2.
3.
4.
5.

What obstacles or distractions do you think will prevent you
from reaching this goal?(including
friends)_____

How will you deal with these obstacles in order to achieve your
goal?

How will you measure your success and track your progress?
(daily or weekly)_____

Did you accomplish your goal?

Yes   Work in Progress   No

Students With Academic Goals
(30 Day jump Start Goal Worksheet)

Day 17

What do you want to
accomplish?_____
(Be Specific)

When do you want to complete it?_____

Why is completing this goal
important?_____

What Steps do you have to take to reach your goal?(Think
about how many steps you need)
1.
2.
3.
4.
5.

What obstacles or distractions do you think will prevent you
from reaching this goal?(including
friends)_____

How will you deal with these obstacles in order to achieve your
goal?

How will you measure your success and track your progress?
(daily or weekly)_____

Did you accomplish your goal?

Yes   Work in Progress   No

Students With Academic Goals
(30 Day jump Start Goal Worksheet)

Day 18

What do you want to
accomplish?_____
(Be Specific)

When do you want to complete it?_____

Why is completing this goal
important?_____   _____

What Steps do you have to take to reach your goal?(Think
about how many steps you need)
1.
2.
3.
4.
5.

What obstacles or distractions do you think will prevent you
from reaching this goal?(including
friends)_____   _____

How will you deal with these obstacles in order to achieve your
goal?

How will you measure your success and track your progress?
(daily or weekly)_____

Did you accomplish your goal?

Yes   Work in Progress   No

Students With Academic Goals
(30 Day jump Start Goal Worksheet)

Day 19

What do you want to
accomplish?_____
(Be Specific)

When do you want to complete it?_____

Why is completing this goal
important?_____

What Steps do you have to take to reach your goal?(Think
about how many steps you need)
1.
2.
3.
4.
5.

What obstacles or distractions do you think will prevent you
from reaching this goal?(including
friends)_____

How will you deal with these obstacles in order to achieve your
goal?

How will you measure your success and track your progress?
(daily or weekly)_____

Did you accomplish your goal?

Yes   Work in Progress   No

Students With Academic Goals
(30 Day jump Start Goal Worksheet)

Day 20

What do you want to
accomplish?_____
(Be Specific)

When do you want to complete it?_____

Why is completing this goal
important?_____   _____   _____

What Steps do you have to take to reach your goal?(Think
about how many steps you need)
1.
2.
3.
4.
5.

What obstacles or distractions do you think will prevent you
from reaching this goal?(including
friends)_____

How will you deal with these obstacles in order to achieve your
goal?

How will you measure your success and track your progress?
(daily or weekly)_____

Did you accomplish your goal?

Yes   Work in Progress   No

Students With Academic Goals
(30 Day jump Start Goal Worksheet)

Day 21

What do you want to
accomplish?_____
(Be Specific)

When do you want to complete it?_____

Why is completing this goal
important?_____

What Steps do you have to take to reach your goal?(Think
about how many steps you need)
1.
2.
3.
4.
5.

What obstacles or distractions do you think will prevent you
from reaching this goal?(including
friends)_____

How will you deal with these obstacles in order to achieve your
goal?

How will you measure your success and track your progress?
(daily or weekly)_____

Did you accomplish your goal?

Yes   Work in Progress   No

Students With Academic Goals
(30 Day jump Start Goal Worksheet)

Day 22

What do you want to
accomplish?_____
(Be Specific)

When do you want to complete it?_____

Why is completing this goal
important?_____   _____

What Steps do you have to take to reach your goal?(Think
about how many steps you need)
1.
2.
3.
4.
5.

What obstacles or distractions do you think will prevent you
from reaching this goal?(including
friends)_____

How will you deal with these obstacles in order to achieve your
goal?

How will you measure your success and track your progress?
(daily or weekly)_____

Did you accomplish your goal?

Yes   Work in Progress   No

Students With Academic Goals
(30 Day jump Start Goal Worksheet)

Day 23

What do you want to
accomplish?_____
(Be Specific)

When do you want to complete it?_____

Why is completing this goal
important?_____

What Steps do you have to take to reach your goal?(Think
about how many steps you need)
1.
2.
3.
4.
5.

What obstacles or distractions do you think will prevent you
from reaching this goal?(including
friends)_____

How will you deal with these obstacles in order to achieve your
goal?

How will you measure your success and track your progress?
(daily or weekly)_____

Did you accomplish your goal?

Yes   Work in Progress   No

Students With Academic Goals
(30 Day jump Start Goal Worksheet)

Day 24

What do you want to
accomplish?_____
(Be Specific)

When do you want to complete it?_____

Why is completing this goal
important?_____

What Steps do you have to take to reach your goal?(Think
about how many steps you need)
1.
2.
3.
4.
5.

What obstacles or distractions do you think will prevent you
from reaching this goal?(including
friends)_____

How will you deal with these obstacles in order to achieve your
goal?

How will you measure your success and track your progress?
(daily or weekly)_____

Did you accomplish your goal?

Yes   Work in Progress   No

Students With Academic Goals
(30 Day jump Start Goal Worksheet)

Day 25

What do you want to
accomplish?_____
(Be Specific)

When do you want to complete it?_____

Why is completing this goal
important?_____

What Steps do you have to take to reach your goal?(Think
about how many steps you need)
1.
2.
3.
4.
5.

What obstacles or distractions do you think will prevent you
from reaching this goal?(including
friends)_____

How will you deal with these obstacles in order to achieve your
goal?

How will you measure your success and track your progress?
(daily or weekly)_____

Did you accomplish your goal?

Yes   Work in Progress   No

Students With Academic Goals
(30 Day jump Start Goal Worksheet)

Day 26

What do you want to
accomplish?_____
(Be Specific)

When do you want to complete it?_____

Why is completing this goal
important?_____ _____   _____

What Steps do you have to take to reach your goal?(Think
about how many steps you need)
1.
2.
3.
4.
5.

What obstacles or distractions do you think will prevent you
from reaching this goal?(including
friends)_____

How will you deal with these obstacles in order to achieve your
goal?

How will you measure your success and track your progress?
(daily or weekly)_____

Did you accomplish your goal?

Yes   Work in Progress   No

Students With Academic Goals
(30 Day jump Start Goal Worksheet)

Day 27

What do you want to
accomplish?_____
(Be Specific)

When do you want to complete it?_____

Why is completing this goal
important?_____

What Steps do you have to take to reach your goal?(Think
about how many steps you need)
1.
2.
3.
4.
5.

What obstacles or distractions do you think will prevent you
from reaching this goal?(including
friends)_____

How will you deal with these obstacles in order to achieve your
goal?

How will you measure your success and track your progress?
(daily or weekly)_____

Did you accomplish your goal?

Yes   Work in Progress   No

Students With Academic Goals
(30 Day jump Start Goal Worksheet)

Day 28

What Do you want
accomplish?_____
(Be Specific)

When do you want to complete it?_____

Why is completing this goal
important?____   _____

What Steps do you have to take to reach your goal?(Think
about how many steps you need)
1.
2.
3.
4.
5.

What obstacles or distractions do you think will prevent you
from reaching this goal?(including
friends)_____

How will you deal with these obstacles in order to achieve your
goal?

How will you measure your success and track your progress?
(daily or weekly)_____

Did you accomplish your goal?

Yes   Work in Progress   No

Students With Academic Goals
(30 Day jump Start Goal Worksheet)

Day 29

What Do you want
accomplish?_____
(Be Specific)

When do you want to complete it?_____

Why is completing this goal
important?_____

What Steps do you have to take to reach your goal?(Think
about how many steps you need)
1.
2.
3.
4.
5.

What obstacles or distractions do you think will prevent you
from reaching this goal?(including
friends)_____

How will you deal with these obstacles in order to achieve your
goal?

How will you measure your success and track your progress?
(daily or weekly)_____

Did you accomplish your goal?

Yes   Work in Progress   No

Students With Academic Goals
(30 Day jump Start Goal Worksheet)

Day 30

What Do you want
accomplish?_____
(Be Specific)

When do you want to complete it?_____

Why is completing this goal
important?   _____

What Steps do you have to take to reach your goal?(Think
about how many steps you need)
1.
2.
3.
4.
5.

What obstacles or distractions do you think will prevent you
from reaching this goal?(including
friends)_____

How will you deal with these obstacles in order to achieve your
goal?

How will you measure your success and track your progress?
(daily or weekly)_____

Did you accomplish your goal?

Yes   Work in Progress   No

S.W.A.G. NOTES SECTION:

S.W.A.G. NOTES SECTION:

S.W.A.G. NOTES SECTION:

S.W.A.G. NOTES SECTION:

S.W.A.G. NOTES SECTION:

EXTRA'S

INCLUDING

Q&A with the author

Q&A WITH THE AUTHOR

How did you come up with the SWAG acronym?

I was speaking at a university in Louisiana about the importance of being a student, when a student said that I had a lot of SWAG. I knew that SWAG meant style, personality, and an abundance of confidence, however I wanted to redefine what it stood for. I pondered for a while and came up with the idea and then created a Seminar called Respect the S.W.A.G. The rest was history, every place I delivered this presentation I received a standing ovation.

What are some of the programs offered by I'm So Educated?

I'm So Educated™ offers dynamic programs geared towards helping students connect the dots to their educational future. We offer peer mentorship, Student Enrichment Programs, and incredible motivational lecturers.

In your own words, what does it mean to be educated?

For one to be educated or if I stay true to my brand "So Educated" it simply means to acquire knowledge, apply knowledge, and share knowledge. If one educates them self often, then applies that knowledge to their everyday life, and finally, once they make it to their level of success or while on their journey to success, they share their knowledge to uplift others, I believe is what being educated is all about.

What are you trying to achieve with this book?

In short I am trying to give students a book that not only speaks to them, but also helps inspire their academic performance. I want students to see that if you want to be successful these are tips that can help you achieve your goal. I just really want to inspire students and help them become the future leaders of our world.

Do you think this book will be well received?

Of course, I am a voice for the students of the world. I know traditionally according to societies standards, someone with a PhD has more credibility, however many students do not connect with adults who they do not feel comfortable with. Respect the S.W.A.G. will be in schools around the world because it speaks to them.

Where have you delivered speeches or seminars at?

WOW!!! Here's a few:

Yale University, University of Connecticut, Hofstra University, American University, Louisiana State University, Southern University and A&M College, South Lake High, University of Houston, National Urban League, INROADS, Bulkeley High School, CT, Northside High School, LA, Nicholls State University, Phi Beta Sigma Fraternity Inc., Central Connecticut State University, Scotlandville High School, Pi Sigma Epsilon Business Fraternity, etc.

Be Featured

Congratulations!!! YOU have officially become the S.W.A.G. Now that you are on your path to success it's time for you to share your story with the world.

To be featured, go to www.imsoeducated.com

Click on *Be Featured* Choose your feature. Tell the world your story!

Made in the USA
Charleston, SC
22 June 2014